ANGELS
HAVE GIZZARDS

A Child's-eye View of Religion

by

Lois Blanchard Eades

Beacon Hill Press of Kansas City
Kansas City, Missouri

ISBN: 083-411-1500

Printed in the
United States of America

Cover Design: Crandall Vail
Cover Illustration: Raoul Soto

10   9   8   7   6   5   4   3   2

To
Eunice, Esther, and Paul—
heirs with me
of a great spiritual legacy

Contents

Preface

Whoever said, "Children should be seen and not heard," was robbing himself of one of life's great satisfactions. A child's view of life may broaden our own—give us insights into the nature of the world we live in and the unseen world that we apprehend only by faith. Faith seems natural to most children, and their curiosity about things of the spirit is unquenchable. When they talk about God and heaven, they should be heard. When they ask questions, they should be answered. When they pray, God listens. And so should we.

Putting together this collection of anecdotes has been a delight. There is no way that I can give credit to all the friends who have shared with me recollections of their own childhood or stories about children they have known. In particular, I want to thank R. Franklin Cook, editor of *World Mission,* for allowing me to use material from the "Wee Wisdom" column, which for many years was a feature of that publication.

Quotations from *Papa Was a Preacher,* by Alyene Porter, copyright 1944, renewed 1972, published by Fleming H. Revell Co., are used by permission.

1

IT'S IN THE BOOK

I don't know whose child it was who arrived at Sunday School with a note pinned to his shirt, "This child's views concerning the Bible do not necessarily reflect those of his parents." But several people I know may wish they had written such a message. For a child's-eye view of the Book may be surprising and original, even enlightening.

A friend of mine was called on to arbitrate a dispute between her niece and nephew. The disagreement had reached a high degree of vocal intensity when little Marjorie finally appealed to her, "Aunt Naomi, weren't there two men in the tree?"

"What tree, Marjorie?" she asked.

"Zacchaeus' tree."

"No, there was only one."

"Yes, there *were* two," Marjorie insisted, "Zacchaeus and Hasten—because Jesus said, 'Make Hasten come down!'"

Speaking of Zacchaeus, twins Janelle and JoAnn had a great regard for his agility. Their kitten climbed a tree, and one of them proposed that they go after it. The other one reminded her, "Daddy says that we can't climb trees."

"Then I'll go and call Zacchaeus," her sister said.

Bible words and names are often strange to young ears. Seven-year-old Ruth, in her Kentucky mountain Sunday School, listened intently as her teacher began to tell the story of Jesus entering Jerusalem on a donkey. "What happened as Jesus rode along?" the teacher asked.

"They threw pomegranates at Him!" was Ruth's answer. To a child who has seen neither palm branches nor pomegranates, what is the difference?

Randy was reading the Bible and stopped to ask his mother, "What is your posterity?"

"It's your descendants," she explained, "the people who come after you."

"Oh," Randy said, "I thought it was back here," and he indicated the posterior portion of his anatomy.

His mother checked to see what he was reading and understood why he was puzzled. It was Amos 4:2, which reads, "The Lord God hath sworn . . . that he will take . . . away . . . your posterity with fishhooks."

Amy Jo had a penchant for substituting her own words for the original. When she recited the first psalm, the man was blessed who does not sit in "the seat of the cornfield." And in Ps. 18:2 the Lord was not her "deliverer" but her "liver."

Mary Beth also created her own version of a familiar verse. She was distressed because she spilled her milk twice during the same meal. Shortly afterward, during family devotions, her parents asked her to recite the 23rd psalm. Her three-year-old mind gave it a new twist that day: "My cup runneth all over the table!"

A small boy who had decided to sit with his Sunday School teacher during the worship service seemed disturbed when the usher came down the aisle to take the offering. He began to pluck at his teacher's sleeve.

"Look!" he said. "He's got a tie on!"

"Yes?" she answered, wondering why the child seemed to disapprove.

"You told us today," he whispered, "we were supposed to bring all the ties into the storehouse."

Jimmy's father helped him to memorize a scripture each night before his bedtime story. For a while they were working on the Ten Commandments. When they came to "Thou shalt not commit adultery," his father remarked to his mother, "I hope he doesn't ask me to explain that one."

Jimmy didn't ask, but his three-year-old tongue had trouble pronouncing words he was not familiar with. So when it came time to recite the seventh commandment, he said, "Thou shalt not commit a-girl-y." His father, who has a few graduate degrees, commented, "I've gone to school 15 years to understand the Bible, but Jimmy understands that at age three."

Bobby at 2½ had difficulty with certain consonant sounds. He said "nake" for "snake" and "neeze" for "sneeze." His parents were constantly drilling him on these words. One day his father quoted in his sermon the verse "The night cometh, when no man can work" (John 9:4).

Bobby whispered to his mother, "What's the matter with Daddy? Can't he say 'snowman'?"

Even when the words come through clearly, a child with a practical turn of mind may have difficulty with the feasibility of certain Bible events. Three-year-old Becky listened to the story of the prodigal son and then asked, "If the father *fell* on the boy's neck, how could he kiss him?"

Angela and Stephen were listening as their mother told them the story of creation. Six-year-old Angela had a question: "If God made us out of dust, why don't we melt and turn into mud when we get wet?"

Before her mother could say anything, Stephen drew an answer from his four-year accumulation of wisdom: "Well, He let us dry for a good long time."

Maybe it is apocryphal, but the story is still worth repeating of the child who was watching a beautiful sunset with his mother. When his mother reminded him that God was the Artist who had painted it, he said, "Yes, and He did it with His left hand."

"How do you know?" she asked.

"Because Jesus is sitting on His right hand."

Bible names! When they give us adults so much trouble, how can we expect the children to cope with them? A friend was teaching a series of lessons on the Book of Daniel to his class of boys. "Who is our lesson about today?" he asked.

"Ne*buck*ashazzar!" answered one of the boys.

While the media bombard us with fictional names and events, it is no wonder that a child sometimes confuses the facts of the Bible with the figments of men's imagination. A minister in a Tennessee community, whose children have been exposed to a lot of Bible, was taken aback recently when his four-year-old daughter, Cameron, asked, "Daddy, do you remember the story about Huey, Dewey, and Louie—and the fiery furnace?" David, twice her age, was more knowledgeable. He knew that the three Hebrew children were Shadrach, Meshach, and a Billy Goat.

One of my childhood favorites was the story of Elijah. I remember squirming with pleasure when Mother would begin, "And Elijah the Tishbite, who was of the inhabitants of Gilead . . ." (1 Kings 17:1). I never asked what a "Tishbite" was, but I had a distinct impression that it had to do with a fish biting.

Aaron's mother was reviewing with him the events we celebrate at Easter and was pleased that her four-year-old recalled accurately the details of Jesus' crucifixion, burial, and resurrection.

"And who was the first person to arrive at the tomb and discover that Jesus was not there?" she asked.

Aaron pondered a moment and then confidently answered, "Mary Magazine!"

Randy at 3½ knew the story of the Good Samaritan but insisted on calling him the "Good American." After his parents had corrected him, he gave the benefit of his new intelligence to his pastor, who preached on the Samaritan *woman*. The Samaritan, he informed the preacher, was a *man*.

Little James was reading to his mother the events surrounding the birth of Jesus. "He took the young child and his mother by night," he read, "and departed into Egg-wiped."

"Son," she said, "spell that last word for me."

"E-g-y-p-t," he spelled—"Egg-wiped."

11

On the other hand, a child sometimes surprises us by being able to pronounce Bible names that give trouble to adults. Three-year-old Melissa had been listening to the story of David on tape until she was familiar with the names of the people who were important in David's life. Walking one day with her parents, she met a man on crutches, whose foot was bandaged.

"Mama," she asked, "does he have an ow-ee?"

"Yes, it looks like he has an ow-ee," her mother answered.

"Like Mephibosheth?" Melissa said glibly. Perhaps if we don't tell them the name is difficult, they will not realize it— another argument for teaching them the Bible very early.

I am not sure it was a child (perhaps an adult with a freakish sense of humor) who first observed that Isaiah had a horse named Ismee. Why else would he have exclaimed, "Whoa, Ismee!"

Fairy tales and stories of the supernatural are part of the daily fare for children. So when you tell them about miracles of the Bible, they are likely to react with less surprise than you expect. They often seem to endorse Walt Whitman's line, "Why, who makes much of a miracle?"

Little Brady at the age of four had a serious interest in the Bible. His pastor encouraged this interest and often talked to him about the Bible. One day when visiting the family, he took Brady on his lap and began reviewing the story of the feeding of the 5,000.

"And when the little boy gave Jesus his five loaves and two fishes," he asked, "was there enough for everybody?"

"No," sighed Brady, "but they made it do."

I remember the first time I read to Kendall, who was about two years old, the story of how the ravens fed Elijah. "They brought him bread and meat in the morning and bread and meat in the evening," I told him.

Kendall looked a little disappointed. "Why didn't they bring him any cookies?" he asked.

Matthew's mother was reading to him from his Bible story book the story of Elijah and the widow who fed him. "How could he ever find the woman who was to care for him?" she read.

"In the yellow pages?" Matthew suggested.

Chad came home from his kindergarten class in Sunday School, trying to tell the story he had heard. Because he was having difficulty, his grandmother and aunt tried to help him.

"Well," Chad said, "Jesus was in a boat asleep."

"And there was a storm?" they suggested.

"Yes," said Chad.

"And the disciples were afraid?"

"Yes."

"So the disciples woke Jesus up?"

"Yes!" Chad was looking at his grandmother and aunt with amazement.

"And Jesus calmed the sea?"

"Yes!" Chad exclaimed excitedly. "Were you two there?"

Young minds are often hazy about when and where the Bible events took place. In discussing a Bible story with one of my own children, I learned that he thought all Bible incidents happened in heaven. Such a view makes the Bible seem very remote from the world the child lives in.

A more serious problem is that we are often tempted to distort the Bible stories and emphasize the sensational at the expense of the spiritual elements of the story simply in order to hold a child's interest. Unfortunately, some children, often influenced by the media, are likely to prefer Bible stories that include gore and violence. When Mother asked, "What Bible story shall I read?" one of us four was almost certain to answer, "Read about where the dogs ate Jezebel." She seldom obliged.

13

The stories that teach deep spiritual and moral truths may take root in young hearts, but we usually have to wait for their flowering. Teaching a lesson on temptation to a group of junior high students, I started with a hypothetical situation:

"You are in a supermarket. You are hungry and you see a display of red apples. You love apples and no one is looking." Then I told the story of the temptations of Jesus, noting that He answered each one with a scripture, including "Man shall not live by bread alone" (Matt. 4:4; Luke 4:4).

"Now," I said, "back to the apples in the supermarket. What scripture could you give Satan for an answer to that temptation?"

They had recently had a series of lessons on the Ten Commandments, so I was confident of their answer. But their originality surprised me. The answer I got was a tentative, "Man shall not live by apples alone?"

Allowed to tell the Bible stories themselves, children can often make them more relevant to their lives than we can. Six-year-old Mark's mother overheard him telling the story of Samuel: "God woke Samuel up three times in the night to talk to him. Then God said, 'You go back to bed, and I'll leave you alone so you can sleep.'"

One father told the story of David and Goliath to his two young daughters and then had them repeat the story to him. One of the girls gave it a dramatic ending: "And then David had giant for supper!"

A teacher was telling the Resurrection story and letting the class help. One small girl informed the rest of the group that three Marys came to the grave—"Mary . . . and Mary Magdalene . . . and Mary had a little lamb!"

Five-year-old Johnny was a most articulate member of a class to whom a teacher was telling the story of Isaac's servant at the well. "What is the one thing you would need most out on a hot desert?" she asked.

"A fan!" Johnny shouted.

After she had established the fact that water might be more important than a fan, she told them how thirsty the man was after his long trip and how he stopped at a well. "Do you know what a well is?" she asked.

"Sure!" Johnny was prompt again. "It's a big fish in the water!"

Steven was a child who not only told the Bible stories but also had to dramatize them. He told his mother one day, "Noah came to visit me. We're going to build the ark." Later he reported, "Well, we launched the ark. Noah sat in the front, and I sat in the back with the animals. His three sons weren't there. They were swimming."

John and Jimmy loved sports—basketball, baseball, and football—but their favorite way of playing was for one to play the game while the other acted as sports commentator. One rainy day they were confined to the basement, where they decided to play basketball. It was four-year-old Jimmy's turn to be sportscaster.

On the evening before, the family had watched an Easter special on television that had depicted somewhat graphically the beheading of John the Baptist. So on this particular morning their mother heard the young commentator announce: "There goes the great John Allan Knight the Baptist dribbling the ball! Uh-oh! He loses the ball, and it goes rolling down the floor! Oh, no, folks, that isn't the ball. It is the head of the great John Allan Knight the Baptist!"

Children find ingenious ways to apply the Word of God to their lives. Three-year-old Robin had been scolded for hitting her friend Paul. A few minutes later, she called from her bedroom, "Mother, I'm reading the Bible."

"Why?" her mother asked.

"So I won't hit Paul anymore."

Rachel's mother announced that her older daughter, Mary, was coming home for Christmas and bringing a male guest.

15

"Who is he?" Rachel wanted to know.

"I don't know," her mother confessed.

"Well," Rachel decided, "if he's coming with Mary, he must be Joseph."

The teacher in a Friday evening craft class said to the children, "All right! Craft time is over. It's time for cleanup. Everyone get to work!"

Third grader Venus said in a tone of resignation, "Yes, ever since Adam sinned, we all have to work."

Roger at the age of six was always being teased by a group of older girls at school. Finally he decided to use the Scripture to call down judgment on them. He defiantly pronounced: "Meanie! Meanie! Tickle you farsin! You'll be judged in heaven for that!"

Eleven-year-old Merion was dreading her scheduled blood tests for hepatitis. Trying to get her to "think positive," her mother said, "The Bible tells us to fill our minds with happy thoughts."

"That's all right for *you*," Merion answered, "but it's *my* blood."

"Stevie," a father said to his 2½-year-old son, "you have a new baby brother. His name is Daniel."

"Frow him to the lions?" Stevie suggested.

Four-year-old Timmy listened to the story of Naaman, who resented being asked to take a dip in the Jordan. A few days later Timmy was walking past an open sewer ditch and commented to his mother. "This muddy old Jordan!"

Nine-year-old Loy, shopping with his mother, saw an air gun that he wanted very badly. On the next Sunday morning in church he wrote his mother a note that read, "Please, may I have that air gun? Over." Turning the paper over, she read, "Ask, and it shall be given you. Matthew 7:7."

Third grader Johnny kissed his mother's cheek before leaving for school in the morning. As she started to stand up, he said, "Wait, Mom! Don't you know the Bible says to turn the other cheek?" She was glad to.

Perhaps one of the strongest proofs of the inspiration of the Holy Scriptures is that they speak to us all, regardless of our age or station in life. The following paraphrase of 1 Corinthians 13 was written by 11-year-old John Benner and demonstrates how a sixth grader can take God's truth and apply it to the situations he faces every day:

If I excel in math and art but have no love, I am nothing.

If I write the best stories, foretell futures, speak the truth, and win prizes for my scientific achievements but have no love, all that is worthless.

If I have faith to face the toughest test or to calm my fears in a tough group but have no love, my faith will not work miracles.

If I give all my bus money to those less fortunate, and though I give all my strength to the church's well-being, but have no love, I am no better off.

Love is patient when third graders hit me, throw hardballs at me, and call me names.

Love is kind when my sister needs help and I gladly help her.

Love is not jealous when you get a Valkery and your friend gets three Voltrons.

Love does not brag when you make the most baskets in the school basketball game. Love doesn't take all the credit but remembers all the team members helped.

Love is not rude when you are listening to a story that's not so great.

Love does not always want to be the center of attention.

Love is not easily angered when your sister bugs you. Love says, "Forget it," and really means it. Love doesn't hold a grudge.

Love does not delight in evil. When you have two choices of clubs to join—one of popular kids who like to hurt other kids and one of not-so-popular kids who like to have fun—the club with the not-so-popular kids is your first and last choice.

In tests, friendships, and talent contests, love always protects, always trusts, always hopes, and always persists.

Love never gives up when you help a lost child whose parents are very hard to find.

Futurism and science fiction will lose their appeal and cease, but love will stick around.

Smooth talkers and even the hardest science will become obsolete, but love won't.

All our earthly knowledge isn't everything—it's only 1 percent of the story.

But when perfection comes, all will become complete and whole.

Since I am a kid, I talk like a kid, but when I am a man, I will talk different.

All we know now is just a part. Someday God will tell us the whole.

No one understands me completely, not even me, but someday I will understand and be understood.

Faith, hope, and love are all great, but love is the greatest.

2

HEY, JESUS!

Kendra at the age of six was afraid of two things: bad dreams and falling out of bed. Every night she asked her mother to pray that these two things would not happen to her—petitions that her mother faithfully made. After the prayer Kendra would always say, "Did you pray that I won't have bad dreams or fall out of bed?"

Finally in exasperation her mother asked her, "Don't you *listen* when I pray?"

"But, Mother, you're not talking to *me!*" was Kendra's answer.

First grader Timmy was learning to read and was given a Bible of his own. His mother suggested that he was old enough to have private devotions. "You can read a verse from the Bible and then pray to yourself," she said.

"Not to *God?*" Timmy protested.

Children accept easily the fact that prayer is talking to God and that God loves them like a father, so we should not be surprised when they talk to Him as informally as to a father. Three-year-old Melanie was saying her bedtime prayers when she suddenly remembered something she had forgotten to tell her mother. "Excuse me, God," she said—and took time out to give her mother the message.

My nephew Stuart at the age of three became restless one day while the family sat in the car, waiting for a heavy rain to stop. "If I ask God to make it stop raining, will He do it?" Stuart asked.

"You might try it," his mother answered.

Stuart rolled down the window slightly and, trying to make his voice heard above the downpour, called, "Hey, Jesus! Slow down!" Strangely, in spite of the unorthodox manner of the request, the rain stopped until the family and all their gear were safely in the house, then continued with full force.

More often, however, children's prayers are an attempt to duplicate what they have heard in grown-up prayers. One toddler, who had heard his elders pray for God to "put His hand" on someone, prayed, "God, put Your hand on Grandma, 'cause she's sick, but don't put Your hand on Pop-Pops 'cause he's not sick."

Every time four-year-old Steve prayed he asked the Lord to "bless the missionaries in the cornfield." His mother tried several times to tell him that he meant "foreign field" and to explain the phrase to him. Finally one day his eyes lit up, and she was relieved that he understood. Shortly afterward, the family was driving in the country and passed a wheatfield. Steve shouted excitedly, "That's the field the missionaries are in!"

My nephew, also named Steve, kept repeating in his prayers, "Help me not to be helpy and prong." When his parents at last realized that he was trying to say, "healthy and strong," they gently corrected him, explaining that we *want* to be healthy and strong, and telling him what the words mean. When he prayed the next time, he said, "Help me to be helpy . . ." There was a long pause. His father opened his eyes to see what the problem was. Steve was looking directly at him.

"Helpy *means* prong," he said. Some of us grown-ups would do well to recognize such redundancies in our own prayers.

The total honesty of children's prayers is enlightening. When their table grace is not confined to "God is great; God is good . . . ," they often reveal exactly how they feel about the food set before them. My youngest son, Stanley, was a finicky eater. One evening he looked over the items available, then bowed his head and prayed, "Dear Jesus, thank You for the raisins in the salad." Then he proceeded to make his meal on the raisins and nothing else.

Three-year-old Amy prayed, "Dear Jesus, I don't like that stuff over there that has the spoon in it—but help me to eat it."

Amy Jo at the same age was asked to say grace before a picnic meal. She bowed her head and said, "Dear Jesus, thank You for this . . ." Then she looked up and said, "I can't pray. I'm learning not to be first."

Four-year-old David was also at a picnic where each of the children was asked to pray a short blessing before the meal. When David's turn came, he refused to pray. Afterward someone questioned him, "Why wouldn't you pray?"

"I lost my audio," David answered.

Brian was at the age where he spent many of his waking hours pretending to be some species other than human. One day after he had crept through the morning as a mouse, he came to the lunch table with his mother and older brother.

"I believe we'll have Mousie ask the blessing," his mother said.

Brian put his hands prayerfully together, shut his eyes, and squealed, "Squeak! Squeak!"

The association of prayer with *not* eating (fasting) is a strange idea to most children. One three-year-old heard her parents discussing a serious need. They finally decided that they ought to resort to prayer and fasting.

"What is fasting?" she asked her parents.

Her mother explained, "That is when you don't eat, and you ask God to solve a problem by working a miracle."

The child was enthusiastic. "Oh, I want to fast," she said, "—after I eat supper."

Little Sharon was trying to explain fasting to her friend Angie. "Do you know what *fasting* means?" she asked. "It means to eat it tomorrow."

Very conscientious children often frame their prayers to include all persons and all contingencies. One small boy prayed for his friend, "Touch Eddie's cold—if he has a cold." My granddaughter Jennifer prays: "Bless all the people in the world who are sick and help them to get well. Bless all of us who are sleeping tonight and help us have a good night's rest. Bless all the people who are working tonight and help them have a good night's work. Keep us all safe and don't let anything hurt any of us. Amen." Such a prayer amounts to a big order—even for God.

Children can learn very young that prayer, like God himself, is a very present help in trouble. Little Dudley, facing a disciplinary session with his father, would suggest, "Let's pray about it first."

A favorite trick with many children is to prolong the nightly prayers in order to postpone bedtime. Brian and his family were enjoying a visit from a doctor-friend of the family, so close that the children called him "Uncle Doc"—at least Doug did. The best Brian could manage was "Uncle Goc." The doctor had come to discuss with their father a speech he was scheduled to make in a few days, but the boys kept finding excuses not to go to bed. At last their mother managed to herd them upstairs and listened to their prayers. Brian prayed around the world and finally, when he could think of nothing else to say, concluded, "And, God, please help Uncle Goc with his peach."

Like adults, children may pray with motives that are not completely pure, but I believe that my oldest son is the only child I have known who used his prayers as a vehicle for comedy. Kendall learned very soon after his brother Dale was born that it was easy for him to get a laugh out of Dale, and his comedy routines were fine with us until they became a part of his bedtime prayers. He would make off-the-wall remarks in his prayer, all the while watching between his fingers to make sure he was amusing his brother. The night he prayed, "Lord, bless Dale and help him to grow up to be an umbrella," we said, "That's it!" We gave him a prayer to memorize and insisted on his saying that prayer for a few months.

The fact is that the family who prays together will sometimes laugh together. I remember the time the cat was sitting on the back of the porch glider, watching us during our evening devotions. On the side of me that was out of Mother's line of vision I patted the sofa in a gesture of invitation. The cat jumped against the window and nearly knocked herself out. My father was often too sleepy to carry out his part of the bedtime prayer ritual. Sometimes he went to sleep in the middle of his prayer. His voice would trail into silence, his head would drop, and we children would snicker until Mother shook him gently and he finished his prayer.

I continued the bedtime prayer pattern with my own children. Stanley was fond of animals, and we got used to his praying for all the cats and dogs in the neighborhood. But one night when my sister and her husband were visiting us and joining in family prayers, Stan prayed as usual, "Bless Mrs. Hague's cat," and then named several other neighborhood pets. I saw my brother-in-law's shoulders shaking and hoped Stan was not aware of it. Unfortunately, Kendall noticed and joined audibly in the laughter. Stan quit praying abruptly.

"Go on and finish your prayer, Stan," I said.

"No!" he answered.

I was afraid his sensitivities might be injured enough that he would be reluctant to pray after this, so I urged him again, "At least say, 'Amen.'"

"No!" He was firm in his refusal.

Groping for some point of persuasion, I said to him, "Then how is the Lord going to know you are done?"

Kendall had the answer: "He can stick a fork in him." That was the end of family prayers for that night.

Memorized prayers are one way to avoid the unexpected and inappropriate elements in family prayer time, but children who pray such prayers often do not know what they are saying or why they are saying it. What goes through a child's mind when he prays, "Our Father, which art in heaven, Harold be thy name"? Ten-year-old Debbie in our Vacation Bible School prayed, "Howard be thy name." Four-year-old Kayla, after learning that her parents had been appointed as missionaries to Bolivia, prayed, "Lead us not into temptation, but deliver us into Bolivia." Judy was three years old when Evel Knievel was making some of his daring motorcycle jumps. She was frightened when she watched him on television and decided she didn't like him at all. She broke up the family devotions one night by praying, "Deliver us from Evel Knievel."

Even the simple "Now I lay me . . ." has had countless variations. My friend's daughter, Elaine, always prayed it in such a singsong way that her mother was not sure what the child was saying. Then one day Elaine said to her, "When I pray, I say, 'Now Elainie down to sleep,' but when other people pray, they say their own names, don't they?"

Alyene Porter, in her entertaining account of her childhood, *Papa Was a Preacher*, says that one of her brothers had a pet rooster named Fie-shi-die. When someone asked the boy why he chose such a name, he explained, "Well, he crows before I wake up, and in our prayer we say, 'Fie-shi-die before I wake.'"

One of the hardest things for young minds to grasp is why God does not send prompt answers to their prayers. Five-year-old Wesley stopped one evening in the middle of his prayer and said, "Mom, God just doesn't answer prayer."

Surprised, she asked, "Why on earth would you say a thing like that?"

"Well," Wesley answered, "I've been praying for five days that God would make me big like my dad, and just look at me."

A friend who picks up a small boy for Sunday School found him very dubious one day about God's ability to answer prayer. "I keep asking Him to do something about my little brother's temper," he said, "but He doesn't do it."

My own daughter, Elaine, expressed a similar skepticism to me one night after family prayers. Her reason? "I've been praying a long time for a baby sister, and I still don't have one."

But children are not natural skeptics, and often their own faith finds a reason for God's delay. In Elaine's case, her oldest brother married when she was 10. Elaine loved her sister-in-law and assured us one day that God had answered her prayer for a sister, after all.

A child's simple faith in prayer is often a rebuke or a surprise to the rest of us. Nine-year-old Paul was on his way to the drugstore with his mother to get some medicine for her throat trouble. "Should we pray about your sore throat?" he asked.

"You pray while I drive," she answered.

Paul closed his eyes and prayed a simple prayer for her healing. "There, Mom," he said, "that ought to do it."

A Sunday School teacher was telling her class that they ought to pray for forgiveness when they have done something wrong. Then, assuming that all of them had something to confess, she led them in a prayer for forgiveness, which they repeated word for word. As they concluded the prayer, one second grade boy looked up and said brightly, "Boy! Do I feel good!"

A Sunday School picnic was being planned, and the children heard their teacher praying for good weather. The day arrived pleasant and cloudless. "Isn't it nice that we have such a perfect day for the picnic?" the teacher commented.

A puzzled little voice asked, "Why not? You prayed for good weather, didn't you?"

A friend of mine was driving through the Cumberland Mountains one dark night with her five-year-old nephew. She saw that a storm was threatening and, without realizing that she was doing it, began praying aloud, "Lord, don't let it rain until I get off this crooked mountain road." The storm broke anyhow and nearly obscured the road. When they finally reached the straight, level highway, the rain stopped.

Little Wilson didn't let it shake his faith. He had an explanation for the mix-up: "Aunt Bea, I think God and the devil traded places."

"Why do you think so?" she asked.

"Well, you kept asking to get off the mountain road before it rained, but you didn't."

Who can say what a child's faith may accomplish? John's mother walked into the living room one evening and saw her four-year-old son kneeling by the sofa. She backed out of the room and waited to hear what he was going to say. What she heard was "Hey, God, are You listening? Please send me a brother. And if You have three brothers up there, I'll take all three of them. Also, please send me a collie dog to be my protector; and if You have a collie cat, my brother could use him for a protector."

A few months later John's mother told him that there was going to be a new baby in the family.

"I know," said John. "God is going to send me a brother."

Afraid that his faith would be damaged if the baby was a girl, his mother said, "Well, honey, we don't know if it will be

26

a brother or a sister. We have to take whatever is on hand at the time."

"I know *you* don't know if it will be a boy or a girl, but *I* do," John insisted. "God *told* me."

"No, honey," his mother argued, "God doesn't tell anyone until it is time for the baby to come."

Still patient with his uninformed mother, John continued to explain: "Mom, God tells *one* person every time. When Jesus was born, He told Mary. This time He told *me*. It's going to be a boy."

A few weeks later John's baby brother was born. His parents suggested that it might be good to have John do all their praying.

Children's prayers sometimes seem to indicate that they have grasped facets of truth missed by their elders. A friend told me about six-year-old Bobby who played in the mud after his mother had told him not to. When he came in with the telltale evidence on him, she sent him to his room to pray about his disobedience. "Did you ask the Lord to forgive you?" she said to him when he came out of the room.

"No," he answered, "I asked Him to help you put up with me."

Three-year-old Todd had endured several spankings for his behavior in church, none of which seemed to have a permanent effect. Finally his mother decided on a different approach. She had a long talk with him about the importance of proper church behavior, then suggested that they pray about the problem. Todd bowed his head and said, "Dear God, please help Mommy to stop getting after me in church."

My friend Gladys heard her four-year-old Robert tell the neighbor something that was not true. She gave him a lecture on the sin of lying and finally said, "When you try to go to sleep tonight, Jesus will pull your toes to remind you of that lie you told."

27

Going to his room to tuck him in, she discovered that he had gone to bed with his shoes on—"so Jesus can't pull my toes," he explained.

To correct the impression she had given him, she put her arms around him and told him that God loved him and would forgive him for lying. They knelt beside the bed, and Robert prayed a simple prayer for forgiveness. He ended his prayer, "And forgive Mommy too. Amen."

My husband attended seminary 70 miles from home, which meant that he spent five days a week in the city while I was alone in the country with two small boys. Kendall seemed to sense the extra responsibility I carried in his father's absence, so he included in his bedtime prayer, "Bless Mama while Daddy's away and help her get her work done."

One night as we finished praying, Dale said to his older brother, "If you think Mama needs help with her work, why don't *you* help her?" I always want to pass his wisdom along to people who make such suggestions as "Let's pray for the starving people in Ethiopia."

The wisdom and earnestness of children's prayers has immeasurable effect on the adult world. My brother's family lamented the fact that they had to spend an unbearably hot summer without air-conditioning. Later, they learned that their next-door neighbor had stood outside their boys' bedroom window and heard the boys pray at bedtime (which would not have been possible if the house had been closed and air-conditioned). As a consequence, the neighbor man resolved to become a Christian so that he could teach *his* children to pray. He has followed through on his resolution, and my brother is certain that there was a divine purpose in their sweltering that summer.

3

ANDY WHO?

"Mom, who is Saybut?" Gilbert asked.

"I don't know. Where did you hear the name?"

"We sing about him in Sunday School—'O Saybut, I'm glad!'"

Let's face it, though. Saybut hasn't provoked nearly as many questions as Andy—because Andy is a real friend:

> Andy walks with me;
> Andy talks with me;
> Andy tells me I am his own.

When a hymn writer releases his creation to the public, he can never be certain how his lyrics will strike the ears of the very young or how his words may be interpreted. Whether or not there is truth in the legend of "the consecrated cross-eyed bear" or "the calf has never yet been sold," it is nonetheless true that children (and sometimes the rest of us) often hear a message not intended by the poet.

My mother used to tell of the visual image she had when the congregation sang:

> Where the angels wait at the golden gate
> To conduct us there to the mansions fair.

She distinctly saw "two ducks upstairs" waddling across the floor.

Little Aaron likes to have his mother sing to him. He asked her one day to sing "that song about the laundry." It took a few minutes of dialogue for her to figure out that he wanted to hear:

>*Jesus! Jesus! Jesus!*
>>*Sweetest name I know!*
>*Fills my every laundry,*
>>*Keeps me singing as I go.*

Aaron's own song interpretations are not always easily recognizable. "What are you singing?" his mother asked him one day.

"Don't you re*neck*erize it?" he asked, a little annoyed at her slowness.

When my brother Paul sang, you had to "reneckerize" the song by the melody. He could sing almost before he could talk, but he never let his lack of familiarity with the words keep him from belting out the tune. He would sing "Jesus! Jesus! Jesus! We have name I know" or "O come, all ye faithful, joyful and carnality." One of his favorites was a Christmas lullaby, which said of the shepherds:

>*There when they found Him.*
>*A-kneeling around Him,*
>*They worshiped in awe at His feet.*

When Paul sang it, they worshiped Him "all but His feet."

Apparently his son Jeff inherited his father's ear for lyrics. At age five he came home from Sunday School, insisting that his teacher had taught them the words:

>*Father, we thank Thee for the night . . .*
>*For rest and food and lov-ee and care.*

My home congregation used to sing a song about the assurance of salvation, which affirmed:

>*I'm no longer in the dark;*
>*There's no tragic question mark.*

31

A friend of mine seemed to find some spiritual meaning in singing it, "There's no traffic place to park."

My friend Martha recalls a song she heard often in her childhood that ended with the lines:

In fellowship with Jesus
I'm happy night and day.

Her three-year-old sister sang it, "I fell in a ship with Jesus."

And what child has not wondered what you are doing when you are "bringing in the sheaves"? Four-year-old Emmie liked to sing it, "Bringing in the cheese." Karen wondered why she never saw her mother "come rejoicing" as she was pulling the freshly dried laundry off the line and "bringing in the sheets." My nephew sang, "Bringing in the sheep." As a child, I pronounced the word *sheaves,* but since it was not in my vocabulary, I sang it with a mental image of someone bringing in the sheep.

When the words are unfamiliar, the child tends to translate them into a better-known idiom. My five-year-old nephew David was probably repeating a command he had heard many times when he ended "Master, the Tempest Is Raging" with the phrase, "Please, be still." Four-year-old Danielle sang, "Giddy-up, old-time religion." Miriam sang the opening lines of "Tell It to Jesus" as "Are you weary? Are you chickenhearted?" And Rondalyn at 2½ sang, "Hallelujah! I'm the glory!" and "The windows of heaven are broken."

Carla, aged four, was learning the chorus "The Wise Man Built His House upon a Rock." Her mother heard her singing, "The rain came down and the suds came up." René, at two years of age, affirmed that "Jesus loves me, shiny nose." And Kathy lifted her voice with the congregation in beseeching, "Lead on, O kinky turtle!"

Sometimes a child may try to make too wide an application of the lyrics. A teacher who was working with children in a craft class served them punch and their favorite dried seeds during a rest period. John accidentally dropped a seed into his punch. He watched it intently for a while, then took the punch cup to his teacher and said, "See! Love didn't lift it."

Certain songs seem to present special problems for children. Modern soap commercials may have made children familiar with the word *brighten,* but my generation had difficulty with the advice to "Brighten the corner where you are." One of my sisters sang it, "Right in the corner where you are." A small boy assured his mother that he had learned a song,

"Fight in the corner where you are." My friend Adrienne says she heard it as "Brighter the corner where you are." And I clearly recall that I thought the song was about somebody named "Bright Ann."

Five-year-old Naomi kept asking her mother, "What is a para*shing* dashore?" She was repeatedly assured that there is no such word. "Well, then," she finally asked, "what does the song mean that says, 'Bring the para*shing* dashore'?" The same song, "Throw a Line," always mystified me with its final admonition:

> Throw a line, throw a line,
> Strong and ample that will bring them to the shore.

I could see someone throwing a line. But how do you "strong an apple"? And if you figured out how to strong an apple, how could it bring anyone to shore?

At home, at school, at church, and on radio and television, children hear songs. Small wonder that the lyrics become confused in their minds. Four-year-old Beth Ann sang:

> Zacchaeus was a wee little man;
> A wee little man was he.
> He called for his pipe and he called for his bowl,
> And he called for his fiddlers three.

One would suppose that such inaccuracies are corrected when a child learns to read, but even the printed lyrics can give trouble, partly because of the way the words are divided into syllables. One beginning reader asked her older sister, "What does this song mean, 'O *pen* my eyes'?"

Adults as well as children often have questions about the line in the beautiful hymn "Come, Thou Fount of Every Blessing" that reads, "Here I raise my Ebenezer." My oldest son, in a Sunday morning worship service when he was about 10, chose the moment just after the singing of the hymn and before the pastoral prayer to ask, "Mom, what's an Ebenezer?"

I wanted to answer him, but how in such a moment does one say, "Well, when Israel defeated the Philistines, Samuel set up a stone to celebrate God's help and called it Ebenezer, 'stone of help'"? Instead, I made a quick decision to give him an absurd answer, figuring that when we got home, he would say, "Come on, Mom, what *is* an Ebenezer?" I touched my elbow and said, "It's your elbow."

As it turned out, he did not realize I was being facetious, and he never asked again. After he was married, his wife asked him the same question, and he said, "It's your elbow." Shortly afterward, she was in a training class at their church where another member of the class asked the identical question. She answered brightly and promptly that your Ebenezer is your elbow and then suffered the agony of embarrassment while someone else explained the meaning of the word. At home she challenged Kendall, "Why did you tell me . . . ?" And the next time they visited me, I faced the resentful inquiry, "Why did you tell me . . . ?" A little lie can go a long way.

Often a child's revision of a song has its own kind of logic. I have known of two children who sang "Blessed Insurance," probably finding more significance in the wrong word than in the right one. Three-year-old Mark gave a new unity of meaning to a well-known children's song when he sang:

Be careful, little hands, what you do.
There's a Father up above,
And He's looking down your glove.

I have heard my friend Jeanette tell how she derived meaning from songs she misunderstood. Her heart was filled with pity, she said, for the aloneness of the Master as she sang, "There's not a friend like the lonely Jesus." And she knew that the way to heaven is a happy one, so it made perfect sense to sing, "When I've gone the last smile of the way."

Joy, another friend of mine, loved rice pudding when she was a child. She sang "Some Rice Tomorrow!" with a firm faith that there would be rice pudding on heaven's menu.

Perhaps the most elaborate reconstruction of a hymn was made by the poet Kathryn Blackburn Peck, who confessed that when she was a small girl she sang fervently:

> *Rock the babies kept for me;*
> *Let me hide myself and see.*

It was her sincere prayer. She planned to have lots of babies. She knew they would come from heaven. So the song was a plea to the angels to take good care of her babies as well as a prayer that she might be allowed to conceal herself behind a curtain and view the scene, making sure that her babies were getting their share of tender, loving care.

Now and then a child may improve a song when he alters the lyrics. The mother who heard her three-year-old Mark singing "The Way in the Manger" realized that the Manger Child is truly the Way and prayed that Mark would one day know the truth of the words he was singing.

4

THIS IS THE WAY WE GO TO CHURCH

It was Promotion Day. Four-year-old Kristi was coming down the hall toward the sanctuary after Sunday School. She met her mother, who asked her, "Aren't you going to children's church?"

"Not till after the commotion," Kristi told her.

That may be a common misunderstanding. A six-year-old boy went home from Sunday School and announced to his parents: "We had a commotion today, and I got a diplomat!"

We sometimes forget how confusing church language can be. One small boy told his mother, "My teacher says that, if we don't come every Sunday, she'll throw us in the furnace." The mother called the teacher for an explanation and found her as perplexed as herself until she finally recalled telling the children that those who did not attend regularly would be "dropped from the register."

One pastor tells about a girl who took seriously his admonition to seek out and help "the sick among us." After several weeks she came to him troubled because, in spite of a long search, she still had not been able to find the creature, "the sick amongus."

Janelle, even at three years of age, was aware of the bloodshed and violence in the world. One day when she heard her parents talking about a bombing that was reported on the news, she commented, "Our preacher says there is a bomb in Gilead."

Even when they hear the words perfectly, children tend to be literalists. I remember having a strong desire in my childhood to take literally the music director's suggestion to "stand on the last stanza." Only the frowning presence of my parents kept me from putting the hymnbook on the floor and planting my feet on the last stanza.

Four-year-old Rachel took literally the language of a stranger who kept addressing her minister-father as "Brother." Finally she said to the stranger, "Do you know my grandfather?"

"No," he answered.

"Then how can you be my father's brother when you don't even know my grandfather?"

And what about that mysterious object "the church board"? Lemuel at age five loved to play church with his sister and grandmother as his congregation. Usually it was a preaching service, but one day after Lemuel had arranged the chairs he announced that this time it was to be a board meeting. His grandmother sat down on a chair, and his sister took her customary seat on the piano bench.

Lemuel immediately protested, "You can't sit there."

"Why not?" she wanted to know.

"This is a board meeting, and that's the board!"

Three-year-old Arnold, whose parents were much involved in the activities of their own church, was fascinated by a church of another denomination across the street from the home of an aunt he often visited. He watched the people coming and going and often asked questions about them.

38

One day his mother decided that his questions gave her a good opportunity to explain to him that there are different denominations with different beliefs. Suddenly she wondered if he even knew the name of their own denomination.

"Do you know the name of *our* church, Arnold?" she asked him.

Arnold had to think a moment, then he answered brightly, "The board meeting church!"

We can wait for them to learn the vocabulary of the church, but we grow impatient for them to learn the rules of church conduct. Children usually know more about these rules than their actions indicate. Three-year-old Judy knew she should not talk in church, but there are times when one simply *must* ask a question. During the pastoral prayer she noticed that her mother was wiping tears from her eyes, so she whispered, "Mama, is God talking to you?"

Her mother nodded and Judy continued, "He's talking to me, too."

"Oh?" said her mother. "What is He saying?"

"I think," Judy answered, "He is saying, 'Sh-h-h!'"

Three-year-old Joey had a chronic case of the wiggles, a fact that often distressed his mother and other members of the small rural church where Joey's father preached every week. One Sunday his mother felt that she could endure it no longer, and in the middle of the morning message she took Joey outside, planning for a laying-on-of-hands ceremony. Clutching him by the shoulder and shaking him, she said, "Joey! You haven't heard one word your daddy has said this morning!"

Joey's answer was quick and frantic: "Yes, I have! Yes, I have! He said, 'He's been dead four days and by this time he stinketh'!" Joey didn't get his spanking that time.

Some children who misbehave in church don't wait until they are away from the crowd to bring pressure to bear on the potential punisher. One small boy who was being forcibly removed from the sanctuary by his father got more attention as he was being carried out than he got by his original misconduct. All the way down the aisle he begged his father, "Don't kill me! Don't kill me!"

I have been unable to learn the identity of a child about whom a similar story is told. His parents were song evangelists, and during his preschool years he traveled with them from one church to another. The procedure was to establish him on the front seat during the opening part of the service while his parents were busy with the congregational music and the special singing. It wasn't always easy for a small boy to sit still during this time, and it was not easy for the parents to deal with the situation when he elected not to sit still. During one service his parents had repeatedly tried to communicate to him that he was being more active than was necessary, but he ignored all their signals. By the time their part of the service was concluded, his father's displeasure had gathered enough momentum that he didn't even bother to sit down when he left the platform. He scooped his son into his arms and started down the aisle toward an exit door. Looking back over his father's shoulder, just as they reached the last row of pews in the sanctuary, the child requested in a loud voice, "Y'all pray for me now!"

Being chastised for misbehaving in church becomes a way of life for some children. Three-year-old twins Ronnie and Donnie were playing church in the living room. Sitting on the sofa, they sang lustily from a couple of hymnbooks. Then one of them stood up and delivered a brief homily on the subject, "Be kie-yet in church!" He concluded his service by saying, "Now let's go home and get our spankings."

One of the most exasperating facts for parents is that, when they *want* their child to be seen and heard in church, the child will often not cooperate. Christina had stubbornly refused to sing or to speak her lines on the Christmas program. Afterward, she wanted to be sure that her perversity had been noticed. On the way home she said to her mother, "Mama, did you hear me not saying anything this morning?"

But even when they try to cooperate, the results are sometimes less than perfect. A group of four small children were performing an acrostic exercise for a Christmas program. Each one carried a letter of the word STAR and recited a verse that featured that letter. In spite of practice and instruction, they marched to the front in reverse order, held up their letters, and announced that they were RATS.

Anyone who has worked with children's groups knows that catching and holding their attention is a most crucial and most difficult part of their Christian education. For several years I was responsible for the children's missionary education in our small church. The children were as young as 3 and as old as 13, and finding a common point of interest was almost an impossibility. For a while, 4-year-old Rachel was my biggest challenge. She was always under the table or on top of it or pestering the other children to divert their attention. So I was most agreeably surprised during one session when, as I told a story, she sat perfectly still and never took her eyes from my face. I wondered, Is this story unusually interesting? What am I doing differently today? Finally, just as I reached the climax of the story, Rachel broke her silence.

41

"My granny," she said, "has wrinkles in her face just like you have."

Children's concepts of the church are often linked to their attitude toward the minister. Five-year-old Donnie was asked one day by his pastor, "Donnie, what are you going to do when you grow up? Would you like to be a preacher?"

Donnie's big blue eyes looked straight into the pastor's face as he answered, "No! I want to *work* for my money!"

Victor's father was a preacher himself and was always proud when his 3½-year-old son said that he wanted to be a preacher. One evening as the minister was cutting a watermelon for a group of guests, he said to his son, "Tell them what you want to do when you grow up."

With no hesitation Victor answered, "I want to cut watermelons!"

My friend Russell was standing near the church entrance at the close of the service, saying farewell to his parishioners. Little Susan stood directly in front of him, facing the people as he shook hands with them. If he moved to the right, she moved to the right. If he moved to the left, she followed. A bystander remarked, "That child really loves her pastor."

"No," Susan corrected him, "my hair is hooked on his coat button."

I cannot vouch for the authenticity of the story my brother tells of a very young lad who was entertaining the preacher while his mother prepared Sunday dinner. "Guess what we're having for dinner," the child said.

"I can't guess," was the minister's reply.

"Buzzard!"

"Buzzard?" The minister sounded skeptical.

"Yes. I heard Mom tell Dad we might as well have the old buzzard for dinner."

It does seem that children reserve their most shocking remarks and their most unseemly behavior for the times when the minister is present. I recall a time when my parents

42

were entertaining a minister of some distinction. My younger sister, who was perhaps three years of age, came downstairs clad in absolutely nothing and walked into the living room where he was sitting. It was the only time she had ever done such a thing, and it was a source of extreme embarrassment to Mother. You must understand that Mother grew up in an age when ladies did not show their ankles, and she classed among her most embarrassing moments the time when I, at the enlightened age of six, turned a somersault for our pastor and showed him my nether garments.

A Sunday School teacher in a church not far from us was occupied one Sunday morning with giving the children their individual parts for the Easter program. While she was explaining their parts to the children at one end of the table, she heard a voice at the other end saying, "One for you and one for you and one for you and one for me." Looking up, she saw that a small girl had brought a deck of playing cards to Sunday School and was expertly dealing them to some of her classmates. Before she could get to the children to take control of the situation, her pastor appeared in the doorway, observing her classroom procedures. She wondered, as we all do at times, why the minister doesn't show up when they are on their good behavior.

My own daughter, Elaine, was expert at saying the thing we least wanted her to say—to ministers and laypeople alike. Our family often went camping during our vacation weeks, and it was a firm rule that we went to church twice on Sunday just as we did at home. But one Sunday, while we were camping in a state park in South Carolina, a heavy rainstorm came just at the time when we should have been getting dressed for the evening service. The children ran for shelter, and by the time the rain was over and we had reassembled the family, it was too late to go to church. The Boy Scouts were having a camporee in the park that weekend, and we found Elaine in a pavilion where the Scouts were dancing. A friendly Scout was teaching her to dance.

That was in August. As I recall, no one mentioned the episode again. Late in the fall our district superintendent paid us an unexpected visit. This was the minister who was our immediate supervisor—a man we were most eager to impress with our integrity. When Elaine came in from her first grade class at school and saw him sitting on the sofa, she walked over to him and with no preliminaries said, "Hello, Dr. Knight! When we were on vacation this summer, we didn't go to church, and *I* went to a dance!"

Those of us whose children like to shock the preacher wonder why they can't be like eight-year-old Brian, who wanted to *impress* the preacher. His parents had invited a church dignitary for dinner, and Brian's mother had tried to give the boys an idea of the ecclesiastical importance of their visitor. She apparently succeeded, for at breakfast time Brian greeted his mother with "Well, Mom, I guess you are *really* excited today. The biggest wig in the church is coming to our house for dinner tonight."

The visitor turned out to be relaxed and charming and, to Brian's pleasure, full of anecdotes and jokes. Since this was Brian's idea of good conversation, he answered each of the minister's jokes with one of his own. Midway through the meal Brian excused himself from the table but returned very shortly. At the first lull in the conversation he said, "Have you heard the one about . . ." The visitor took him up on it, and the chain of stories started again, each one trying to outdo the other. Finally one of his parents noticed that Brian was sitting with his head down during the stories their guest was telling and realized why Brian had left the table. His joke book was carefully concealed under his napkin. He was not going to let anyone else, even "the biggest wig in the church," tell the last joke.

If they don't disgrace us with what they say *to* the preacher, it's what they say *about* the preacher. Four-year-old John had been taught by precept as well as by the example of his minister-father that one who wants to keep his body clean and healthy will not smoke cigarettes or use tobacco in any other form. He was listening to the network news with his parents when the historic surgeon general's report was aired, linking cigarettes to lung cancer. The next Sunday John reported to his teacher, "Did you know that my daddy doesn't smoke cigarettes anymore? He wants to have a clean body, so he smokes a pipe since the report."

For some reason the minister's child seems to be held more responsible than other children for what he does and says. Many preachers' children would sympathize with the son of a minister-friend of ours who was overheard saying, "We haven't got a chance! Our father is a preacher, and we're supposed to be good; and our mother is a teacher, and we're supposed to be smart. We haven't got a chance!"

The teacher of the kindergarten group in our Sunday School reported to me one Sunday that our Elaine apparently felt a similar pressure. Because she was more articulate than most four-year-olds, the teacher often addressed questions to her. On this particular Sunday she must have asked one question too many. Elaine answered vehemently, "I don't *know!* Just because I'm the preacher's kid, you think I'm supposed to know everything."

Today's children are influenced by movies and television and often associate elements of church life with what they have learned from these media. A friend of mine took a small boy to church for the first time and observed that he was wide-eyed when the offering plate was passed. "I didn't know you had to *pay* to go to church," he whispered.

Another boy, attending church for the first time, gave his opinion that the music was OK but the commercial was too long.

At the advanced age of five, Jason thought that he was old enough to stay at home from Sunday School if he wished. When he realized that he was going to be forced to go, he said, "Well, I'll go this Sunday, but when they start having reruns, I'm quitting!"

My brother, who is in aeronautics research, was teaching a class in Vacation Bible School. One day their lesson was on vocations, and he asked the children about their plans for their lifework. One boy expressed his interest in being a scientist.

"Good!" said Paul. "That's what I am."

"No, you ain't," the boy contradicted.

"Yes, I'm a scientist," Paul insisted.

"Well, then," he asked, "why ain't I never seen you on television?"

During a similar discussion I had with a class of younger children, one small girl had a difficult time deciding what she wanted to be. After the usual responses from the other children—"Teacher," "Preacher," "Mother," "Doctor"—she suddenly broke into a cherubic smile. "Oh, now I remember," she said. "I'm going to be a fan dancer!"

One of my friends was preaching a sermon on the power of God. "What else," he earnestly asked his congregation, "can give you such power?"

Five-year-old Rusty shouted, "Cheerios!"

Joshua at five years of age loved the "Gomer Pyle Show" and especially the gruff Sergeant Carter, whom he often tried to mimic. One Sunday when the pastor was preaching and dropped his voice for special effect, Joshua's voice came from the rear of the sanctuary in a clearly recognizable imitation of his hero: "I can't *hear* you!"

But if children tend to associate church with their experiences of the secular world, they sometimes do the opposite—interpret other areas of life in light of their knowledge of the church. The first time we took our oldest son to a basketball game, he stared with disapproval at the fans who were consuming popcorn, hot dogs, and Coke and demanded to know, "Why are all these people eating in church?"

Three-year-old Leslie sat in the car with her mother, watching a policeman direct traffic. He pointed one way, then another, then lifted his hand straight up. "Mama," she asked, "is he preaching?"

Even children who attend church regularly understand only gradually the various rituals and procedures of the church. Melody was just two when she attended her first wedding. Watching the bride come down the aisle, she asked loudly, "Why is she wearing that curtain on her head?"

Another girl, after seeing her first wedding at the age of four, gathered her friends in the yard and organized a similar ceremony. Her mother watched the scene through the window and later asked, "What were you playing?"

"Wedding," she answered.

"Who was the bridesmaid?"

47

"Nancy."

"Who was the best man?"

"Tommy."

"Who was the bride?"

"Well, *I* was."

"And who was the groom?"

"Oh, Mom," she said, "we didn't have any groom. We just wanted a *small* wedding."

Amy Jo at seven had seen healing services in the church where the elders observed the scriptural injunction to pray for the sick and anoint them. She asked her father, "When you pray for sick people, do you use oil or vinegar?"

But it is the absolute newcomers who give the church services that really special flavor. One small boy who attended church for the first time and watched the ushers hand out bulletins to the adult worshipers said in a plaintive voice, "*I* want a menu."

Three-year-old Kevin watched his newly converted father enter the waters of the church baptistry with the pastor and announced to the congregation in a loud voice, "That's my daddy, and he's scared!"

Steve, who pastors a church in Memphis, shares the story of two boys who attend his Sunday School but seldom stay for morning worship. One Sunday when they decided to stay, Steve was having a Communion service. When the congregation came forward, he noticed that the two boys came and knelt with the other communicants. Because he knew they were unfamiliar with the ritual, he kept his eye on them. At the moment when Steve read the sacred words, "This is my blood . . ." and invited the worshipers to partake of the cup, the two boys turned to one another as if on a signal, struck their Communion glasses together, and said, "Cheers!"

5

BUT WHERE IS HE?

"Why can't I see Him?" When children ask this question, it is not usually an expression of doubt. But in a world where seeing and hearing and touching are so important, an invisible God is hard to comprehend.

Some children seem to accept easily the fact that He is there although they cannot see Him. Three-year-old Victor was afraid in the dark, but shortly after his mother and sister assured him that God was with him, they passed by his room where he lay in bed in the dark and heard him say, "Hi, God!" The next day he announced, "I'm not afraid in the dark anymore. God is with me."

But for Wesley at age 2½ the assurance of God's presence was not so comforting. After his mother had put him to bed, she heard him call frantically, "Mother! Come in here!"

When she answered his call, he said, "My animals are coming alive!"

"We'll take them out," she said and carefully removed all his stuffed animals from his room. A few minutes passed and he called again, "Mother! Come in here!"

"Yes?" she inquired, going into his room again.

49

"There's somebody in the closet." His mother turned on the light and let him search the closet before she left the room again.

"Mother!" he called again. "Come in here!"

This time there was someone under the bed. So she turned on the light again, and they checked under the bed.

Then she heard him again, "Mother! Come in here!"

Exasperated, she went to his room and said, "Wesley, there's nobody in this room with you but Jesus, and He's here to protect you."

"Well, get Him out!" Wesley ordered her. "I don't want anybody in this room but me!"

Many children want more than a simple verbal assurance that God is present and real. They would like to see Him. The church is the house of God, so why shouldn't they see Him there? A group of children in Vacation Bible School were taking a tour of the church building. Finally one small boy said, "God sure has a big house—but I haven't seen Him anywhere."

One Sunday evening Wyn, age four, came to visit his grandmother. "Did you go to Sunday School this morning?" she asked him.

"Sure did," Wyn replied. "But Jesus wasn't there. I reckon He was out walking on the water."

It should bring God closer when we tell the children that He can be in their hearts, but the child with a practical turn of mind often sees this as a physical impossibility. Many of them wonder, as two-year-old Ann did, "How can Jesus be in my heart and in heaven too?"

Heather at about the age of four asked her father, "Daddy, does Jesus *live* in your heart?"

"If you're a Christian, He does," her father answered.

"Does He *eat* there?" Heather wanted to know.

50

I heard Dr. James Dobson tell about a small girl riding in the car with her mother who asked, "Mother, is Jesus in your heart?"

Assured that He was, the child got on her knees and laid her head against her mother's chest.

"What are you doing?" her mother asked.

"I'm listening to Jesus in your heart."

They rode in silence for a while; then her mother asked her, "Well, what do you hear?"

"It sounds like He's making coffee in there," her daughter told her.

At what age should a child come to realize that this "heart" is not the red pump in his chest? I have known two adults who were perturbed over the religious implications of heart transplants. One woman asked me earnestly, "What if they replaced a Christian's heart with the heart of someone not a Christian?" How can we expect 5 to understand what 50 cannot comprehend?

Four-year-old Tim was told that God is "above the clouds." Shortly afterward he made an air trip to Japan. He watched carefully from the window of the airliner until it had climbed above the clouds and then challenged his mother, "Mom, there's the clouds, but I don't see Jesus."

Children have an idea that things "above the clouds" are not quite the same as here. Drew had never been anywhere in his two years without being buckled up by a seat belt. One day he asked, "Does Jesus live in the sky?"

"Yes, He does," his father replied.

"Then He doesn't have a seat belt," Drew affirmed.

Some children seem to take comfort in the idea that God is at a distance. Seven-year-old Larry used a word that was forbidden in his home. His mother said, "God will get you for using ugly words."

Larry confidently assured her, "He *can't* get me. He's up there, and I'm down here."

But more often children are troubled at the thought of an all-seeing God. Unfortunately, some adults use this fact to control a child's behavior. I remember a stern woman with a harsh voice who conducted children's services in my home church. She taught us a song complete with gestures:

> He sees all you do;
> He hears all you say;
> My Lord's a-writing all the time.

It took several years for me to erase from my mind the picture of a vindictive God following me with His accusing eyes and recording with robot gestures my every peccadillo. Consequently, I was determined not to give my children the same impression of God.

Kendall was scarcely three when, sitting in his father's easy chair one day in a meditative mood, he suddenly asked, "Can God see me all the time?"

I knew of no honest answer but "Yes."

"Can He see me *now?*" he persisted.

"Yes," I repeated.

He thought about his predicament for a while, then came up with a solution that had never occurred to me when I was dreading the divine omniscience. "I'm going to shoot God," he said.

Kelli, age five, found an explanation for God's awareness of our behavior in the fact that He is "holy." He watches us through these holes. "God is really holy," she said. "He has lots of holes. He sees everything. He always knows what you are doing."

We try to teach them to balance the idea of a just God with the picture of a loving God. And for a child whose parents use love and discipline wisely, the two concepts can exist together. Four-year-old Kirk asked his parents, "Does Jesus spank little boys?"

"No," they said. "Jesus loves you."

52

"*You* love me," he reminded them, "but you spank me."

Little Rachel found a way to use to her own advantage the assurance she had been given of God's loving care. She wanted to go to the ice-cream parlor, but her grandmother objected that she was too young to go alone. "I won't be alone," she promised. "Jesus is with me."

Five-year-old Craig was also sure that Someone was watching out for him. He had spent four years in Jordan and was getting ready for Christmas in the United States. His grandmother teased him, "Do you think Santa Claus will be able to find you in your new home?"

"I'm not worried," Craig assured her. "God will give him all the facts."

We can teach children to recite, "God is a Spirit" (John 4:24), but we cannot keep them from visualizing Him in a physical form, usually much like the pictures they have seen of Jesus. Three-year-old Carla saw a bearded man and firmly maintained that she had seen Jesus that day.

A young couple who were alumni of Memphis State University returned to their alma mater for an important football game, taking their young son with them. Their pleasure in the day's events was spoiled somewhat by a downpour of rain. Crossing the campus after the game, they met a heavily bearded student. The child ran to him, looked up at him accusingly, and said, "God, why did You make it rain?"

The bearded man stepped gracefully into his new role. With a princely bow he assured his questioner: "The trees needed a drink."

Whoever God is, He is the supreme Authority, especially to children who have been taught respect for authority. "Miss Susie," who directs a Christian kindergarten, listened to an argument going on in one of the play centers.

"You're not my boss!"

"I know. Miss Susie is."

53

"No, she's not! [Well, Miss Susie wondered, who *is* then?] God is."

"No, He's not! [Now Miss Susie really gave heed. Was there a higher authority yet?] God *and* Miss Susie are the boss."

Miss Susie could relax, confident that she was part of a good managerial team.

Children have a way of giving back to us what we have taught them about God—but sometimes with a new twist. Three-year-old Debbie knew that Jesus belongs to everyone, so she expressed this faith in her own version of the pledge to the Stars and Stripes: "with liberty and Jesus for all."

Kendra, age six, was asked to keep an eye on her new baby brother, who was lying in his infant seat. Fearful of the responsibility, she asked, "What if he falls out?"

"He won't," her mother assured her. "I trust you."

"You *do*?" Kendra was surprised. "*I* trust Jesus."

Three-year-old Nita climbed into bed with her parents and snuggled up to her doting father. "Who's the best daddy in the world?" he asked her.

"God is," she replied.

Her father gulped and tried again. "Sure, but after God who's the best?"

"Jesus is," Nita answered.

He figured her next answer would be the Third Person of the Trinity, but he had to find out. "Well, then, after Jesus who's the best daddy in the world?"

"Oh, Daddy," she said, "you know it's *you*." He accepted third place, grateful that his child had learned to believe in a loving Heavenly Father.

Among my eldest son's early attempts at writing verse was the following gem. We accepted it as comic verse and only realized after we had wounded him with our laughter that he apparently meant it as an attempt to affirm the Lordship of Jesus.

54

Slopmore was a good old king,
  And he reigned and had his day,
And the day he died was no day to sing,
  So the people didn't get there way.

Slopmore the Second was the king's son.
He ruled the kingdom just for fun.
The people didn't like Slopmore,
So they tied him and hung him at a poor man's door.

Don't let your son try to be king of all.
Let Jesus be king one and all.
And if your son's growing up to have fun,
Just tell him what poor Slopmore done.

But in their mixing of the sacred and the secular and their searching for the reality of God, children sometimes seem to have moments of clearer vision than ours. The parents of three-year-old Linda were searching for a place to live, praying for direction, but not having any success. They had arrived almost at the point of panic. One morning, after they had prayed as usual for guidance, Linda asked, "Are we going to help Jesus find us a home today?"

Her parents suddenly realized who was in control. They relaxed and committed it into His hands. Incidentally, they did find a home that day.

Not all children are so comfortably confident of the divine care and presence. The Easter season was just over, and four-year-old Kayla, who had seen Jesus portrayed in several Easter pageants, said, "We're sure going to miss Jesus."

And it is still true that some children do not know who Jesus is. A small girl in a kindergarten car pool in Orlando, Fla., was reporting on her birthday party. One of the other girls complained, "I never get to have a birthday party because my birthday is on Christmas."

"But just think," said the mother who was driving that day. "You get to share your birthday with Jesus."

"Jesus?" commented one of the five-year-old boys. "He's not even in this car pool!"

Children have no difficulty in believing that God is Creator. All things have to be made by someone, but it is not always easy to decide which ones are made by God. One mother was asking her two-year-old twins to name the things that God has made. They began with the usual list: "Birds . . . flowers . . . fish . . . people." There was a pause, then one of them suggested, "Heinz Ketchup?" Three-year-old Christina expressed her gratitude that God has made bubble gum.

But children are not grateful for all of God's creation. Daryll, age four, awoke on November 1 to find that the ants had invaded his trick-or-treat booty. "Don't you wish," he asked his brother, "God wouldn't make ants?"

Five-year-old Brandon in Tennessee apparently thought he could improve on God's layout of the earth. He loved to go to Florida and couldn't understand why they didn't make the trip more often. "Why did God make Florida so far away?" he asked.

Kim's four-year-old mind through a process of analogy arrived at a strange conclusion about creation. She knew that God makes trees and flowers and that the factory makes shoes and dresses. So there are two creators—God and the factory. She was also taught that God disapproves of certain kinds of behavior. One day when she was scolded for being naughty, she asked, "Why? Doesn't the factory want me to do it?"

Many children arrive at their own explanations of how God makes rain and snow or thunder and lightning. My six-year-old granddaughter Jennifer, who seems to have something of the poet in her, described snow as "crumbs of white bread falling from angels' plates." My early explanations of natural phenomena were more prosaic. I remember thinking that the thunder sounded like Mother's rolling pin on her worktable, and during a thunderstorm I was sure that hundreds of rolling pins were rolling across the sky.

My niece Marilyn, who lived in Guatemala, often watched the girl who helped with their housework as she washed the kitchen floor. She let the water fall between the wide floorboards into the toolroom beneath. Marilyn confidently informed her brothers that, when it rained, God was washing the floor in heaven and letting the water fall through the floorboards. "And when it thunders," she added, "God is moving the furniture."

Her friend Rudi had a different explanation. He loved to stand on the porch and enjoy the storms. One day he ran inside and called, "Daddy! Hurry up and come outside! God is taking pictures! I just saw His flash!"

Four-year-old Erin, when lightning struck closer than usual and the thunder was deafening, said, "Wow! God must have liked that one. He clapped loud!" And Rosanna at the same age apparently thought there was a message in the thunder. One day lightning struck the storage building next door to their house, and when the thunder subsided, she said, "Yes, God, what do You want?"

So God is Creator. But how does Jesus fit into the picture? If you have ever tried to discuss the Trinity with a child, you will sympathize with the mother who tried to explain it to her small daughter Allison.

"Mommy," she asked, "are there two Men up in heaven—Jesus and God?"

Her mother sat down. "Now, Allison, I know this is not easy for you to understand, but the answer to your question is yes—and no. There is God and there is Jesus, but they are one and the same."

Allison pondered for a long moment and then said, "Mommy, that's the craziest thing I ever heard."

We have to realize that they "know in part" (1 Cor. 13:12) and that it is our responsibility to help them to a more perfect understanding. Two small cousins of mine, three and seven years of age, were overheard by their mother in solemn conversation.

In a shocked tone the younger one asked, "Jesus is *dead?*"

"Yes," his mentor informed him, "He is dead."

"I *loved* Him," said the three-year-old. "What happened to Him?"

"Well," answered the voice of authority, "I haven't read my Bible much lately, so I can't tell you. But He's dead."

Always we hope for the day when they will experience the reality of God although we cannot explain the mystery. Melissa was three years old when her pastor decided to have family Communion at Christmastime. The pastor's wife set up a table on the platform in the sanctuary, with a lovely tablecloth, a centerpiece, and candelabra. Christmas music played softly in the background as each church family met separately with the pastor and his wife for Holy Communion.

Melissa's mother tried to explain to her what it would mean—that it was a time to be very close to God and that, in fact, He would *be* there with them. When it was her family's turn to go in, Melissa was awed by the transformation of the sanctuary. But while the pastor was getting ready for the sacrament, she whispered to her mother, "When is God coming? Where will He sit?"

"We can't *see* Him," her mother said, "but we can *feel* Him."

The next time she looked at Melissa, the child was waving her arms in the air and grasping with her fingers. "*I* can't feel Him," she said.

Troubled that Melissa took her words so literally and wanting the experience to be meaningful, her mother tried again: "If you sit very still and think about how much God loves you, you will feel Him in your heart."

The ceremony was lovely and, for the children's sake, was purposely kept simple. When it was finished, the pastor bent over, picked Melissa up, and hugged her. She looked at him and said very solemnly, "God *was* here. I felt Him all warm in my heart."

6

OLD MAN/NEW MAN

Robert's mother thought it was a heavy idea for a seven-year-old when he asked, "What if I'm not really in this body and am just dreaming I am?" Even very small children seem to have some intuitive knowledge that there is a distinction between flesh and spirit.

I was probably no older than three when I first became aware that my spirit (Mother called it my "soul"; she wasn't into the dichotomy/trichotomy controversy) will exist somewhere forever after this body has returned to dust. "Only your soul goes to heaven," Mother assured us. But how does a three-year-old conceive of pure spirit in a world where everything is experienced by the senses? Heaven, for me, became a place heavily populated by "souls," but they were not invisible. They were white, vaporous, and translucent, oblong and hardly two feet high, and they moved silently along the golden streets on very short, thin legs.

Angels, too, were spirits—ministering spirits, Mother said—but for me they had more substance than this mysterious "soul" that was within me. Still, since they could appear and disappear, I thought of them as somewhat less dense than this "too, too solid flesh" of mine.

My sister Eunice must have had similar difficulty in distinguishing flesh from spirit. She was watching Mother cut up a chicken one day and was asking her to identify the parts.

"Do I have a gizzard?" she asked.

"No," Mother said, "only creatures with wings have gizzards."

"Oh," Eunice decided, "then angels have gizzards, I know."

Separating "heart" from "soul" was not easy either. They told me that my soul needed to be saved, but when it was, Jesus would come into my heart. My heart was black, I learned, and would become white only after Jesus came in. I envisioned a literal area of inky darkness within my chest. Sometimes I meditated on how embarrassing it would be to have any sort of surgery that would reveal to the outside world this internal uncleanness.

John, at eight years of age, was able to carry this "grime" metaphor to a solution. He asked his mother, "Do you know the dirtiest place about us?"

"Where do *you* think it is?" she asked.

"Our hearts," he said. Then he quickly added, "But God has the best washing machine in the world."

This blackness, I knew, came from the fact that the devil was in my heart—or "the old bad man," as Mother called him (I think her dislike of the word *devil* came from the use of the word in profanity). To complicate matters still more, Mother spoke also of "the old man." This creature was not to be identified with "the old bad man." The "old man" was the original sin nature mentioned by Paul in Eph. 4:22 and Col. 3:9. When we were angry or stubborn or disobedient, Mother would say, "That's the old man in your heart."

One day Eunice posed a serious anatomical problem: "Mother, what would happen if the old man got out of my heart and got into my stomach?" Mother passed her query along to our minister, who commented, "That would be a big stomachache!"

At any rate, whether internal or external and by whatever name, the enemy was awesome. He was to be avoided and resisted. I could never have shared the emotion of six-year-old Lee when he visited Hell's Canyon in Idaho. He became very upset when the family decided to leave. "We can't go now," he protested. "We haven't seen the devil yet." But not for me! I had heard of people who had seen him, and the thought was frightening.

Six-year-old Gwyneth recognized the role of the enemy in her life when she prayed, "Dear Lord Jesus, will You please try to kill the devil? It's him who makes me naughty."

To children in evangelical churches the vocabulary of sin and salvation often becomes familiar before they know the meaning of the words. Amy at the age of four attended a church where the pastor often "opens the altar" during his pastoral prayer, inviting members of the congregation to come forward and pray about their special concerns. One Sunday morning her father, who sings in the choir, noticed that Amy came to pray along with her mother. On the way home he questioned her, "Amy, I noticed you came to the altar this morning. What were you praying about?"

"Well," she responded with great deliberation, "I asked the Lord to take away my sins—and give me some new ones!"

Cindi at the same age knew the vocabulary well enough to turn it to her own advantage. While she was playing outside the house, her mother, looking out the kitchen window, saw her do something she had been forbidden to do. She called her inside and asked her why she had disobeyed.

"But, Mother, I didn't do it," Cindi said.

"I *saw* you do it," her mother insisted. "Don't make it worse by telling a lie."

Again Cindi denied. "Cindi," her mother told her, "I'm more concerned about your telling me a lie than about your disobeying me."

"Oh, Mother, you don't have to worry about me," Cindi answered smugly. "You know I haven't come to the age of accountability yet."

Her mother reported the incident to her father and said, "You're the preacher in this family. *You* deal with it."

So he took Cindi into his study and set her on his desk. "Now, Cindi," he said, "what does 'the age of accountability' mean?"

"Oh, Daddy," she replied, as if she couldn't believe he would ask a question with so obvious an answer, "that's when you know the difference between right and wrong."

Daddy pointed his finger at his four-year-old daughter and said, "You're there!"

The answer to the problem of whatever is wrong with the heart is to be "saved," and we teach them this word early. An elementary school teacher was discussing with her class the various things that people collect. "Some people save stamps," she said. "Some save books, buttons, pennies—"

One six-year-old, whose father was an evangelist, raised his hand. "My father saves people," he volunteered.

Six-year-old Gay was sitting in her mother's beauty shop, watching an electrical repairman, who happened to be also the pastor of a local Freewill Baptist congregation. As he worked, he was reporting to Gay's mother on the revival in progress at his church. Among the converts the previous evening, he told her, was her own brother Claud, who was Gay's favorite uncle. Some minutes later her mother found her sitting in rapt meditation in a back room. "When I grow up," she told her mother, "I'm going to get saved in that Three-Wheel Baptist church just like Uncle Claud."

I recall one of my less successful attempts to teach the concept of saving grace. I was asked to work with my sister in a series of morning children's meetings held in a tent where a home mission campaign was being conducted at night. Many of the children came from unchurched families, and Eunice was determined to share with them everything there is to know about the good news of salvation. She stressed the fact that merely being good and going to church every Sunday would not save them. She used visual aids and object lessons, even a jar of inky water to represent the sinful hu-

64

man heart. After explaining confession and repentance, she dropped into the jar a chemical that cleared the water.

There was, however, a black button still in the jar, which represented, she told them, original sin, or *carnality* (she had them repeat the word). This, she explained, we inherit from Adam, and it is the cause of all the evil that emerges from the human heart. No one could accuse Eunice of not being thorough.

My role throughout the week was simply to sit there and quell any disturbances that might occur. Since the children were usually quiet and attentive, there was little for me to do. You can imagine my dismay, then, when we arrived on the last morning and Eunice said to me, "I want to quiz the children today and find out whether they know what I've been talking about. I'll take all of them who are of school age. You take the preschoolers and quiz them."

So, with no time for preparation, I stood before a group of three-, four-, and five-year-olds to give them a final examination in soteriology.

"If you're good boys and girls and go to Sunday School every Sunday, will you go to heaven?" I asked them.

"Yes!" they all chorused.

I tried again. "Now wait. Just being good won't take you to heaven. If you want to go to heaven, you have to be—" I paused and waited for the magic word *saved*.

Four-year-old Chapman, the pastor's son, supplied the missing word. "Dead!" he shouted.

Well, I reviewed the lesson on being saved, then moved cautiously to the lesson on original sin. They'll never remember the word *carnality*, I thought, but I had to try. "What is it in our hearts," I asked, "that makes us do bad things?"

"It's a button!" Chapman announced. And that was the end of the quizzing session.

Object lessons can often convey truth that is difficult to teach in the abstract—but sometimes with unexpected results. A minister who loved to work with children was trying to teach them a lesson on faith. "Would you believe me," he asked the group of children, "if I said I could jump over this church?"

"No!" came a cynical voice.

"Yes!" said one wide-eyed, trusting child.

"Would you believe me," the minister continued, "if I said there's a man outside sitting on a fireplug and giving away quarters?"

"No!" said the same skeptic.

"Yes!" said the believer.

"Good!" said the minister. "Go outside and get the quarters." The trusting one left while the scoffers pitied his gullible nature.

In a few minutes the believer returned with his faith rewarded. He had a handful of quarters, received from a man previously planted by the minister to fill the role. Uncomfortably and enviously the skeptic eyed the handful of riches, then said to the minister, "All right, Smartie, let's see you jump over the church!"

R·GREEN

Perhaps we complicate the Good News for children by object lessons and metaphors. The simple idea of praying for forgiveness when they have done wrong is something they can grasp at an early age. Three-year-old Robin and his pup got into the chicken yard and chased the baby chicks. By the time they were discovered, more than half the chicks were dead. Robin's brother Jim, one year older, decided that his little brother needed to pray about his misdemeanor. The two boys knelt together and Jim prayed. When they stood up, Jim asked, "Now are you sorry?"

"But why is it bad to chase baby chicks?" Robin wanted to know.

"I think you need to pray some more," Jim said and forced his brother to his knees again.

Becoming a Christian may seem easy, but *living* the Christian life can be a demanding thing for a child—unless one can simplify it as four-year-old Debbie did. During devotions the family was discussing the distinguishing marks of a Christian.

"I'm a Christian," said Debbie.

"How can people tell you're a Christian?" her mother asked.

"Because I'm so cute," was Debbie's answer.

Three-year-old Mark was also serenely confident of his standing with God. He asked his mother one day how one goes to heaven and listened as she tried to explain in simple terms what one must do to be a Christian. When she had finished, he said, "I don't have to do any of that. God and I settled it before I got in your tummy."

Children can be stern moralists. Maybe they learn from us adults to judge the rightness or wrongness of a person's heart by what he does or does not do. Kendall was only two years old when we first heard him pronounce judgment on a fellow human being. We were having lunch in a restaurant, and a woman at the table next to ours lit a cigarette. Kendall remarked quite audibly, "Look at that women smoking a cigarette. She's going to hell!"

Cindi's criterion for what makes a Christian was perhaps somewhat more accurate. It was Christmas Eve, and to her great delight Santa came to see her. He sat in the living room and visited with the family for a while. Cindi sat beside him and carried on an animated conversation with him. Noticing his watch, she said, "My papaw has a watch just like yours, Santa." At this point Santa became a little restless and said he thought he had better leave.

Wanting to detain him as long as possible, Cindi suggested, "Let's have a word of prayer before you go, Santa."

But Santa said, "Not this time. I really am in a hurry." And he left.

A few minutes later Cindi's grandfather came in (having shed his disguise). Cindi ran to him and said excitedly, "Santa was here!" Then she added with a look of real distress, "But, Papaw, Santa's not a Christian. He wouldn't even pray before he left."

Another concept that we grown-ups can unwittingly pass along to children is that one can unbecome a Christian as easily as he can become one, perhaps more easily. My friend Esther says that she remembers very early in life hearing people talk about "backsliding." She pictured it in her mind as a rather interesting game, somewhat like leapfrog, and wondered why it was frowned upon.

Six-year-old Miriam thought it would be convenient to have a Christianity that could be put off at will. She was passing a town carnival with her mother and had been told that Christians don't attend such affairs. "I wish I wasn't a Christian, Mother," she sighed. "Then I could go to the carnival."

I remember a great deal of talk about backsliding when I was a child, and I had a vision of God perched like a bird on a twig, ready to fly away and leave me backslidden if I made one wrong move.

But out of this dread came one of my most cherished childhood experiences. I was kneeling by my bed, consumed with this fear and beseeching One whom I saw as a reluctant God not to abandon me. Then an inner voice assured me, "I will never leave thee, nor forsake thee" (Heb. 13:5). I didn't know where to find the words, but I knew they were God's words. I stood to my feet in a state of exhilaration. I had heard many people testify that God had given them a promise, and the realization that I had received my own promise was more heartening than I can say. God thought I was "people."

7

WHAT COMES AFTER?

Heidi had not heard much about death until she was three years old. When her good friend, Mr. Joe, died, she had more questions than the family could answer. All right, he was in heaven, but how did he get there? She finally decided that he must have grown some wings before that final flight. She wanted to be assured that he was with Casey, her departed St. Bernard, and with her cat that had been killed on the highway.

Then just about the time that she was reconciled to his being happy in a far-off paradise, her grandfather took her to visit Mr. Joe's grave. The questions began again: "Is Mr. Joe under those flowers? How can he be there and in heaven too?"

Probably a child's ideas about death grow largely out of the way adults react to it and talk about it. For some children it is a frightening idea. My niece Marilyn, however, saw it as an enviable experience. The first time she was taken to see an acquaintance lying in a satin-lined coffin, surrounded by soft music, banks of beautiful flowers, and friends who obviously loved her, she was so impressed that for days she kept saying wistfully, "I wish *I* was dead."

My friend Jeanette tells of going to a funeral home where little Stephen, a very young victim of cancer, lay in his casket. Someone introduced her to Jason, a blind boy who was a friend of Stephen. She sat down beside him, wondering what to say to a child who has had the double misfortune of being blind and losing a friend. She didn't have to worry. Jason himself kept up the conversation. "Stephen has gone to a new home," he told her. "And when I get there, I can see and I can run! I'll run right up to Stephen and say, 'Hello, Stephen! How are you?'" Perhaps children can teach us something about how to face the reality of death.

Jennifer, my eight-year-old granddaughter, gave a unique interpretation of death. "Some people," she said, "think God is a shepherd and we're His sheep. I think He's more like a fisherman and we're His fish. He's sitting on the bank of heaven with His fishing line hanging down. When it's time for us to die, He just hooks us and pulls us up to heaven."

Four-year-old Christopher asked, "Do people shut their eyes when they die?" Assured that they do, he said, "Well, when I die, I'm not going to shut *my* eyes!"

"Why?" his grandmother asked him.

"Because I want to see God the minute I get there!"

A friend of mine was trying to clarify the idea of death for her granddaughter, who was concerned about the mechanics of being transported from one realm to the next. "Your whole body doesn't go to heaven," she explained.

"Oh?" her granddaughter asked. "Just your arms and legs?"

The finality of death is a difficult idea for young minds. Children find it easy to believe in resurrection because they want very much to believe in it. A child who loses a family member or a pet often dreams and really hopes that the lost one will come back to life.

Joel was sitting on the floor with his grandmother and gave her a playful push. She fell over and lay very still. He watched her for a while and then asked his mother, "Is she dead?"

"I don't know," his mother answered. "You pushed her pretty hard."

After several minutes during which his grandmother had not moved, Joel decided to escape his problem. He wandered downstairs to where his grandfather was working. But either remorse or curiosity brought him back. When his grandmother heard him coming, she fell over again and lay still as before.

"Is she really dead?" By now Joel was concerned.

"Remember the story of Sleeping Beauty?" his mother suggested. "When the prince kissed her, she woke up."

Joel leaned over and gave his grandmother a long, loving kiss. She stretched her arms slowly, opened her eyes, and said, "Wow! I've just been kissed by a handsome prince!"

Joel jumped to his feet and ran downstairs again. "Grandpa!" he called. "Grandma rose from the dead!"

Chad was just two when he lost his grandfather, and he did not want to believe that his good friend was gone for good. "Grandma," he asked one day, "when is Grandpa coming back?"

"Grandpa won't be back," she assured him, "but we will go to live with him someday."

Chad appeared to be in deep thought for a few minutes. Then he asked, "Where's Grandpa's car?"

"I couldn't drive it," said his grandmother, "so I let Uncle Jim take it to Oklahoma with him."

"Well," Chad informed her, "that's why Grandpa can't come home. He doesn't have a car."

Children can ask questions about death that have troubled the minds of philosophers. When six-year-old David lost his baby brother, Timmy, he wanted an explanation.

"Mother," he said, "you always tell us that death comes because of sin. Now you know good and well that Timmy didn't sin. Why did he die?"

Children can also make beautiful and comforting remarks about death. When I lost my husband, my nine-year-old nephew, Steve, asked his mother, "Why did Uncle Craig die?"

"Well," she answered, "his heart just gave out."

Steve pondered this for a while and then said, "I know why Uncle Craig's heart gave out. He gave a little piece of it to everybody he knew."

Of course, the way to avoid death is to be alive and ready when Jesus comes. This, too, is an intriguing idea for children. I recall being terribly afraid that He would come and I would not be ready, but many children who are confident of their relationship with the Lord seem eager for the big event. Marilyn Hilliker in a *Decision* article tells about her 3½-year-old niece, Carrie, who listened to the choir sing "He's Coming Soon" and then asked her mother, "Is Jesus going to come today?"

"No one knows when Jesus will come," her mother answered, "but the Bible says we should always be ready."

Carrie said urgently, "We've got to go home and pack our clothes."

Seven-year-old Miriam had heard someone talk as if the end of time was right around the corner. She said to her mother, "I won't go to school tomorrow, will I?"

"Well, I guess so, Miriam," her mother answered. "Why wouldn't you?"

"I just thought I might not get home in time to go to heaven," Miriam explained.

Four-year-old Rachel was impatient for His coming and kept asking her mother, "When is Jesus coming to get us?" Finally she suggested, "Maybe we can all go outside together and stand by the trash container and call Jesus very *loud!*"

But probably most children are like four-year-old Melanie and would prefer that He wait awhile. It was Christmas Eve and the family was having devotions. The discussion turned from Jesus' first coming to His second coming.

"Are you ready for Him to come?" Melanie's mother asked her.

"No, I want Santa Claus to come first," she said.

Melanie's older sister, Stephanie, on the other hand, saw the second coming of Jesus as a way out of trouble. She had been promised a spanking, and her mother found her in her bedroom, earnestly praying that the Lord would return before she had to face her punishment.

One of the strangest ideas about the Second Coming that I have heard came not from a small child but from a student at least 16 years of age in a literature class I was teaching. As a background for a story we were reading, I briefly summed up the legend of the Wandering Jew: As Jesus was carrying His cross to Calvary, He tried to rest before the home of a Jew, who drove Him away with curses. Jesus told him, "I am going to die, but *you* will not find a grave. You are doomed to wander the earth until I come back again."

At this point in the story Barbara commented, "I thought He came back every Easter."

But whether we go by way of death or the Rapture, the destination is heaven, and children can tell you all about it. Because we teach them that it is a perfect place, most of them think of it in terms of the very best they know on earth. Four-year-old Chapman, who loved horses better than anything else, assured me, "I'm going to heaven and ride horses."

For Dale at about the same age the most important items were toys. If we were going somewhere he had never been, his first question was always, "Do they have toys?" So it was natural that he should ask me one day, "Do they have toys in heaven?"

74

"There will be children there," I said, "so I suppose there will be toys." This assurance not only made heaven more attractive for him but also furnished him with an answer to the question we frequently asked him about his imaginary friend, Ruthie Guy.

"Why can't we see Ruthie Guy?" we would ask.

"He's up in heaven, playing with Jesus' toys," Dale would tell us.

Four-year-old Christopher had a similar concern. He was going through a period of fascination with play dough and asked his grandmother one evening if there is play dough in heaven. She told him there might possibly be. After a quiet moment he told her with a sparkling smile, "Guess what, Grandma? Jesus just told me in my heart I could bring my play dough to heaven."

Aaron was upset when he saw his three-year-old brother Andy killing a cricket. "Andy," he said, "don't kill that cricket!"

"But I want to," Andy insisted. "I want to kill him so he'll go to heaven, and I'll see him when I get there."

My sister Eunice, who inherited Mother's antipathy to dirt, was distressed because her youngest son, David, considered dirt the most important element of his playtime activity. Dirt was good for making roads and buildings, and he could not understand his mother's aversion to it. He asked her one day, "Are there trees in heaven?"

"Yes," she said, "the Bible mentions the tree of life and the trees that bear all manner of fruit."

He had her! "Then there must be dirt in heaven!" he exulted.

She wasn't ready to concede. "I don't know," she said. "I really can't imagine dirt in heaven."

"Then I don't want to go there," David decided.

Kevin's family was discussing heaven and wondering what kind of clothes we will wear when we get there. Finally they agreed that we will probably wear white robes. Kevin, who for his entire nine years had been a kind of "dust magnet," sighed and said, "I'll probably get mine dirty with gold dust."

Chad attends a Christian school where the classes have regular Bible study. One day his first grade teacher was talking to the children about the beauties of heaven, and the children were becoming excited over the prospect of seeing them. Finally Chad raised his hand eagerly.

"Yes, Chad," the teacher said, "what is it?"

"I'm going to take my camera!" Chad declared.

Occasionally a child becomes so enthusistic over heaven that he wants to go immediately. Four-year-old Emmie on the way home from church asked her mother, "Are we going anywhere today?"

"Just home," her mother said.

"Well, why don't we just go to heaven today?" Emmie suggested.

Beth, at the age of four, was standing by her mother at the close of a moving and meaningful church service. The pastor had called the congregation to the front of the sanctuary and asked them to join hands and sing as an invitation:

Oh, who will come and go with me?
I am bound for the Promised Land.

Beth looked up at her mother and asked, "Is this for real, or is it make-believe?"

Her mother assured her, "This is for real."

"I'll go!" Beth volunteered.

Matthew's friend had died, and his mother tried to soothe his grief by telling him what a wonderful place heaven is. She must have succeeded almost too well, for that night when Matthew prayed, he said, "Help me, God, not to get so excited when I get to heaven that I fall down and hurt myself."

But the average child would, no doubt, agree with the boy we have all heard about who failed to raise his hand when the teacher asked, "How many of you want to go to heaven?"

Surprised, the teacher said to him, "Don't you want to go to heaven when you die?"

"Oh, sure, when I *die*," he answered. "I thought you were making up a load right now."

I found recently among my souvenirs this seriocomic view of heaven, written by my daughter when she was about 12 and titled "My Heaven." It reveals a preoccupation, typical of that age, with food and weight as well as a tendency to see the afterlife in terms of what we cherish here.

When I get to heaven
  I'll be the happiest girl!
Everything will be just lovely,
  My hair and its every curl.

I'll run to meet my Savior
  And sit upon His knee.
Although I weigh 110 pounds
  He'll smile right down at me.

Before the day is over
  I'll find my mansion dear.
When I think of that castle to myself
  I'll almost shed a tear.

The next day I'll look up Jesus again
  And tell Him all my fun.
I won't sit on His knee because
  By then I'll have gained a ton.

After lunch I shall take a little walk
  Around the whole city fair.
It might take a week to see the whole place,
  But I sure don't give a care.

I'll stop to look when I get to town.
  I'll look in dress shops and such.
There'll be little money in heaven
  So I can't buy anything much.

Then I believe I'll go for a swim,
  But I'll find I've forgotten my suit.
There are plenty of other things to do
  Like rob poor Matthew of all his loot.

Everything in heaven will be perfect:
  Food, weather, nature, and smell.
It'll all be just luscious.
  Sure glad I ain't going to hell!

8

MISSIONARY IMPOSSIBLE

Keren had lived only seven years and was just beginning to learn some of the strange facts about the world she lived in. When someone told her that cows are worshiped in India, she giggled. "Do they moo in church?" she wanted to know.

In the book *Papa Was a Preacher* Alyene Porter tells how her father prepared the children for the visit of a missionary from China. Among other things he told them that, if they dug straight through the earth, they would come out in China. In the days that followed, his children tried a little digging but stopped for fear of coming to a region of fire and fiends. The missionary arrived, delivered his message to the congregation, and then asked, "Are there any questions?"

"Yes," said Gil, one of the preacher's sons. "Did you have to go through hell to get to China?"

Little Rodney heard his parents refer to his grandparents as "missionaries." "Are they *missionaries*?" he exclaimed. "I thought they were *Christians*!"

The word *missionary* can conjure strange images for children. For me it was snakes. I seem to recall that, whether he was from India, Africa, or South America, the visiting missionary always told a snake story. Snakes were one of my great terrors, and I earnestly hoped that God would not ask me to be a missionary.

Five-year-old Bobby was left one evening in the care of a neighbor. When his mother returned, she asked him, "What did you do?"

"I watched a really great show on television," Bobby told her. "It was called 'Missionary Impossible.'"

For missionaries and their children the shift to a strange culture can seem almost impossible. Tommy had helped his parents pack food to send to India during a famine. Later his parents were appointed as missionaries to Africa. When they told Tommy about it, he asked in horror, "Does this mean we are going to be hungry too?"

Amy and her baby brother Jay had to be vaccinated for smallpox before their family left for their mission assignment. Someone asked Amy, "Did you get your smallpox shot?"

"Jay got the small one," she answered. "I got the *big* one."

Misti's parents were appointed to Malawi when she was three. She heard her mother explain to people that Malawi was next to Mozambique. One day her mother heard Misti tell a friend that the place where they were going was next to "Nose and Beak."

Eight-year-old Scott was watching his mother pack and label boxes before the family departed for Chile. "What does M-I-S-C stand for?" he wanted to know.

"Miscellaneous items," his mother answered.

"Oh?" he asked. "Is she going to Chile with us?"

Nicole, whose grandparents were missionaries in Chile, missed them and often inquired about them. One day when the four-year-old was asked to say grace, she prayed, "Dear Jesus, bless Grandma and Grandpa in Chile and while they are eating it."

Having arrived at their destination, MKs (missionaries' kids) need time to adapt to new customs. Tommy and Todd were five-year-old twins newly arrived in Swaziland. During prayer time in their first church service, they were amazed to hear the Swazis all praying aloud at the same time. Then suddenly they all stopped at the same time.

One of the boys said to the other, "What happened?"

"I don't know," his twin replied. "I guess their batteries must be dead."

My niece Joyce spent her childhood in Central America. One day when she was about five, a small boy showed up in their Sunday School without a stitch of clothing on. Exerting her authority as part of the missionary family, Joyce went to his older sister and ordered her to take him home and put some clothes on him. The sister took him by the hand and departed. When they returned, the boy was dressed—in nothing but a pair of shoes.

Sometimes adult missionaries must adapt to the customs of the children at the mission site. A new missionary was teaching Okinawan first graders from non-English-speaking homes how to pray in English. She was not quite accustomed to their reciting in unison at the top of their voices.

"Dear Jesus," she said.

"DEAR JESUS!" they shouted.

"Can't you be a little more quiet?" she suggested.

"CAN'T YOU BE A LITTLE MORE QUIET?" they repeated. The prayer lesson was started over with additional explanation.

For parents and children alike, learning a new language is a difficult hurdle. Often it is easier for the children than for the adults, but they sometimes confuse the two languages. The mother of two-year-old Billy in Costa Rica was coaxing him to take some medicine for his upset stomach. He described his dilemma very concisely: "Mouth, no . . . tummy, si."

Spanish uses the same word, *dedos*, for fingers and toes, which was confusing to three-year-old Andy in Ecuador. While his mother was bandaging his wounded big toe, he begged her, "Don't squeeze the thumb of my toes."

Four-year-old Lindsey in Israel was used to hearing language that she could not understand. One day when her one-year-old baby sister was babbling, she said, "I don't understand you, Erin. I don't speak Hebrew."

Billy's parents were concerned because some of the Swazi words he was learning were not socially acceptable. One word in particular that he was forbidden to use was a clucking sound similar to the sound Americans make to express disgust. One day when his mother had forgotten something, she expressed her feelings with this "Tsk! Tsk!" sound.

Billy looked at her closely. "Did you say that in English or in Swazi?" he asked.

MKs even have to adjust their prayers to their new environment. Ten-year-old Gary, after a frustrating first day in his new school, began his bedtime prayer as usual, "Dear Jesus, thank You for the good day and give us another one like it tomorrow." He paused and added, "Well, not *just* like it."

Five-year-old Becky, who had moved from apple country in New York to Costa Rica, prayed from habit, "Thank You, God, for apples . . . Wait a minute! I don't *have* any apples. Well, thank You for the apples I used to have."

John, who arrived in Taiwan when he was six, missed American food. He prayed one day before the meal, "Thank You, God, for the good food. It's better than nothing."

When Ricky moved from Canada to India at the age of 3½, he wanted to be sure God knew where he was. So he added to one of his prayers, "And, oh yes, God, we have moved to another house."

Children of missionaries often feel a responsibility for helping to carry on their parents' work. David, whose father was a missionary in Japan, thought he was old enough at five to distribute tracts. His father gave him a handful and he departed. He was back very shortly, empty-handed and happy.

"Did you throw them away?" his father asked.

"No, I put them in everybody's mailboxes."

"Those boxes are only for mail," his father told him. "The postman won't like that."

"I'm not working for the postman," David assured his father. "I'm working for the Lord!"

I am not sure whom seven-year-old Joyce was working for. She was asked one day to tell a story in a Guatemalan youth service. Her missionary parents, my sister and brother-in-law, sat at the rear of the sanctuary and listened in consternation as she told the entire story of "The Three Bears."

The parents of Laurie felt that their three-year-old daughter was making a quick adjustment to missionary service when she came home from church their first Sunday in Jamaica and announced that she had taught her Sunday School class a new song. Later they learned that the song was "Ring Around the Rosie."

Because of regular furloughs and deputation services while they are at home, MKs get used to a mobile existence, although they sometimes express a wistful desire for more stability. Four-year-old Deborah, watching her mother pack for furlough, asked, "Mother, will we have to pack to go to heaven?"

Daniel, who had traveled with his missionary parents 13,000 miles in a motor home during one summer, was asked, "Where do you live?"

"We don't live," he answered. "We just travel around."

Six-year-old Shelley in Zimbabwe asked, "Daddy, where were you born?"

"In California," he told her.

"Well," she commented, "you got to grow up where you were born. I don't get to. I'm growing up all over the world."

Coming home may be a treat for some MKs but a trauma for others. Melody at 4½ was preparing for furlough. Her mother reminded her, "People will probably ask you to speak Spanish. Will you do it?"

"No!" she said. "And I'm not going to preach either."

Five-year-old Robert not only looked forward to furlough but also looked for an excuse to remain in the States with his grandparents. He finally announced his strategy: "Dad, God didn't call *me* to be a missionary to Peru. He's calling me to be a missionary to the States, and when I get there, I *have* to stay."

After a few years in a different culture, home is a strange place to a child. Christina's mother looked forward to her child seeing snow for the first time. It must have reminded

Christina of popcorn, for when the fluffy flakes began coming down, she called, "Hey, Mom! It's popping out all over!"

Just after four-year-old Warren returned to the States from Belize, his mother bought him a hot dog. "I don't want that!" he insisted. He watched with suspicion as his mother took a bite of hers and then asked, "Mommy, is that the tail?"

Carla had not been home from Bolivia very long before she fell in love with gum machines and wanted to put a coin in every one she passed. Watching her mother put a nickel in a parking meter one day, she asked, "Mommy, what did you get?"

Emmie was three and had just come home on furlough when she saw her first water-skier. "Daddy, come quick!" she called. "There's a man out there on the water chasing a boat!"

Returning to the States, small children are likely to interpret what they see in the light of the culture they are used to. One missionary on furlough stayed in her brother's room, where she could hardly find space for her own belongings because of his treasures, including an impressive array of basketball trophies on the dresser. Packing to return to her mission assignment, she said to her five-year-old son, "Hand me the things from the dresser."

In a scandalized whisper he asked, "The idols too, Mommy?"

But to most MKs their way of life seems the normal way. Amy, while in the States, was playing at the home of one of her friends. She became curious about the identity of the woman of the house. "Are you her mother?" she asked, pointing to her friend.

"No, I'm her grandmother."

"How can you be her grandmother?" she questioned. "You live in the same country!"

But, in a sense, all the children live in a different country from ours, and the messages we get from this country are sometimes funny, sometimes poignant, but always worth listening to.